PROCRASTINATION

Learn How to Become More Productive and
Stress Free by Overcoming Bad Habits and
Laziness

By K. Connors

TABLE OF CONTENT

INTRODUCTION

Procrastination is the habit of putting off or delaying an action or task to a much later time. This word was originated from the Latin pro, meaning "forward, forth or in favor of" and crastinus, meaning "of tomorrow". Procrastination is considered by many as a negative attitude and a counter-productive habit. With that being said, it is seldom viewed in a positive light.

However, procrastination's positive form, as the subsequent historical analysis specifies, is only secondary in usage. Like the rest of common-language terms outlined into scientific study, definitions for procrastination tend to be almost as abundant as the people researching this topic. At the outset, such variation in definition may seem to complicate the nature of procrastination; but in a way, it may also serve to partially illuminate it. Let me explain..

The different attempts by many researchers to refine the understanding of its meaning are more complementary rather than contradictory. Moreover, any common idea only uncovers a core or essential element. It is obvious that all definitions and conceptualizations of procrastination identify that there must be a postponing, delaying or putting off of a task or decision, in keeping with the word's Latin origins.

Based on this, a procrastinator is someone who delays starting or completing a course of action or task. This distinction is relevant, as there are hundreds of tasks that one could be doing at any time, and it becomes burdensome to think that one is putting them all off.

Procrastination nowadays is particularly widespread. Everybody seems to be inflicted with it. It is like a modern disease that knows no race, sex, age or boundary. Some of us may put off tasks every now and then; but for many, it is a way of life to them. In a more recent study, an estimate shows that 80%-95% of college students procrastinate and approximately 75% deem themselves procrastinators, where almost 50% describe themselves as chronic procrastinators.

The total amount of procrastination among students is substantial. It typically takes over one-third of their daily activities, often acted out through sleeping, playing games, social media browsing, or watching TV.

So why do so many people procrastinate? Are we just born this way? I believe the answer is a big NO. We become conditioned procrastinators. One of the reasons is that we fail to look at what causes procrastination. Those seeking to stop procrastination need to first identify the root causes. Only when you know the why, can you make the changes to overcome procrastination.

PROCRASTINATION STATISTICS

Figures on procrastination basically involve the use of statistics, normally utilized in organizations for gathering information on the number of procrastinating workers. This would help the organization to find the causes affecting their profits and the reasons as to why workers procrastinate. It is already well known that procrastination is a term which states the person will defer a task for a later period, which should have been performed at a current period. There are many reasons as to why people prefer to avoid these tasks, which we will cover later on.

Although a person can indulge in procrastination at any point in time, there are high probabilities of occurrence of procrastination at the approach of a deadline. More so, procrastination can also occur during odd moments as well. On some occasions, it may also happen even before a person understands why they're even procrastinating in the first place.

ROUGH ESTIMATIONS

Based on a few local studies, it is estimated that as much as 95% of people are prone to procrastination. Amongst them, 20% of them are chronic procrastinators (this study is separate from that of the college student survey earlier). These individuals have an increased chance of losing their jobs, having financial problems, and having serious problems in their relationship with others.

In addition, when experts do have statistics on procrastination at hand, they can formulate theories as to why a person embarks on this procrastination journey in the first place. Although, it is known that anxiety is the leading cause as to why people procrastinate, there are still many other reasons behind procrastination. It is essential to have a serious look at procrastination, as it affects both the individual and the organization where he or she works or studies.

CHAPTER ONE

WHAT IS PROCRASTINATION?

1.   PROCRASTINATION CAN BE DEFINED AS DEFERMENT OF ACTIONS OR TASKS TO A LATER TIME.

We can say fundamentally that procrastination is the act of putting off the essential task until a later time. Most of the time, non-essential tasks are done in lieu of the more critical ones.

Psychologists term such behavior as a mechanism for coping with the anxiety associated with starting and completing any task or decision.

Usually, the behavior of a person procrastinating is:

Counterproductive

Needless

Delaying

Issues concerning procrastination are anxiety, low sense of self-worth, and a self-defeating mentality.

Procrastinators basically have a lower-than-normal level of conscientiousness.

The approach is mostly based on the "dreams and wishes" of perfection contrary to a realistic appreciation of their obligations and potential.

2.   PROCRASTINATION IS A HABIT, BUT THE GOOD NEWS IS - LIKE ANY OTHER HABIT, IT CAN BE BROKEN.

If unchecked this habit can have serious consequences on our life as well as the lives of the people who surround us.

Procrastination becomes dangerous if further unchecked as it can affect the mental and physical health of the individual.

Here are some suggestions to help you get started and stop procrastination:

Realize that the task to be done is to be done - there are no alternatives.

Self-reflection will help us to determine our personality and know why we are avoiding the particular task. Is it simply our self-defeating behavior or lack of knowledge? If so, learn the task and do it.

Use positive words instead of negatives, as words have meaning and they impact us.

Being confident of our information, equipment and time limit ensures that the task is done on time.

Making realistic expectations and prioritizing on the tasks keeps us well focused on the goals.

Motivation and rewards can self-help us in accomplishing the tasks efficiently.

Let us beat the habit of procrastination with a quote from Napoleon Hill - "Procrastination is the bad habit of putting off until the day after tomorrow what should have been done the day before yesterday."

COMMON CAUSES OF PROCRASTINATION

Most people would admit to having been plagued by procrastination at some point in their lives. A small amount of procrastination, if it only happens sometimes, is normal.

To some people though, procrastination is a cruel habit that prevents them from fulfilling their daily duties effectively, causing them to fail at achieving their career goals. Procrastination happens when there is a gap between when a person is supposed to do a task and when he or she actually does it.

When you find yourself dropping more important tasks in favor of an easier, less important one, then you are procrastinating. The reverse is not the same.

Choosing a more important task over a less important one may just fall under good prioritization. Knowing the causes of procrastination can help you fight this habit and avoid it from becoming a chronic condition for you.

CAUSES OF PROCRASTINATION

1. LACK OF ORGANIZATIONAL SKILLS.

One of the most common among the causes of procrastination is a lack of organization skills. Most people procrastinate on a task because they have not figured out how important the task is. Organized people find it hard, if not impossible to procrastinate because they use such tools as To-Do lists that show how important tasks are relative to others.

They also have schedules that tell them when they need to start certain tasks in order to finish them on time.

2. GETTING OVERWHELMED

Another cause is a feeling of being overwhelmed by a task and fear of success. This happens particularly when your boss gives you a big project without telling you how he or she wants it done. Your boss is leaving the details up to you because he or she trusts that you are equal to the job. Do not let your boss down.

To fight being overwhelmed, break down the project into small, manageable tasks. This will help you get started.

3.   FEAR OF SUCCESS

A fear of success may be causing you to procrastinate. If you are afraid of the consequences of successfully finishing a task, you might procrastinate on it. You may be afraid that you will be given more additional work if you succeed on this one, or maybe be reassigned to another department that needs your skills. Whatever it is, recognize that procrastination will not help further your career either.

4.   BEING A PERFECTIONIST

Another cause of procrastination is being a perfectionist. Perfectionists procrastinate because they dwell on the fact that the perfect circumstances for a perfect outcome do not yet exist. So, they put off a task because they cannot do it perfectly today, or they do not have the perfect resources. Surprisingly, perfectionists are imperfect this way.

5.   LACK OF DECISION-MAKING SKILLS

Lack of decision-making skills can also cause you to put off tasks. If you do not know what to do, you will put off doing it. An example is wanting to move to another job but not knowing what kind of job you want to move to. It will result in you procrastinating on sending in your applications.

Congratulations, you are now better-equipped to recognize and battle procrastination, now that you know the cause.

Procrastination is a very common problem that can lead to increased stress levels, lost opportunities, heightened frustration, and ultimate failure. To effectively overcome this problem and increase your chances of a more productive and successful life, you first need to understand the common causes of procrastination

REASONS WHY PROCRASTINATION ISN'T HEALTHY

1. PERSONAL CIRCUMSTANCES

If you repeatedly set back household chores or relationship duties, such as pitching in with washing the dishes or cooking, disposing of and taking out the garbage, then your marriage life and other relationships may suffer. You may think it's a slippery slope, but these circumstances do in fact occur, sometimes on a daily basis.

2.   GIVES YOU NO INNER PEACE

Another reason why procrastination is bad is because it takes away your inner peace. You are always late for appointments or meetings; you are always hurrying out the door, applying makeup in your car, calling or texting while driving on the road, and in fact risking your life and of those around you. It may seem like an easy thing to postpone, such as dental appointments; however, the instant your cavity gets worse and you miss a day of work with your significant sales presentation, you drop that client and your expectations for a promotion, then you'll realize why procrastination is not good.

3.   HURTS YOUR RELIABILITY FACTOR

Yes, procrastination hurts your reliability and credibility. If your friend needs something from you, your character may be so tarnished that he or she may not rely on you in a time of need. Your best friend may have gotten sick and needs to pick up their kid from elementary school, however, they may possibly think twice before asking you for a favor because they know you may not punctual or will be indecisive until school is almost out. You may be thinking that's a good thing, but just keep that in mind for the next time you need a favor from them.

HOW TO OVERCOME PROCRASTINATION

There is no solution for procrastination except to take action. Taking the necessary action when required to is the only solution there is. Most people procrastinate when it's time to go to the gym or work out, but in fact report feeling better after going to the gym or exercising. Whenever you procrastinate, you are left feeling guilty and even depressed at times. People who lack the motivation to accomplish even minimal tasks have been found to be borderline depressed or manically depressed. You will always feel better after you get things done.

Procrastination adds to depression and can cause one to experience bad health, bad relationships, failing grades, and poor work performance which can lead to the loss of one's employment. No one wants to experience these things happening to them, so why do they procrastinate?

A. RECOGNIZING PROCRASTINATION

The first step in overcoming procrastination is acknowledging that procrastination exists. You can't fix the issue until you first recognize that you have a problem. It's kind of like having a medical issue. You cannot get the needed treatment that's required until you first acknowledge and diagnose the issue, then you can move on to treating the problem.

The following are several symptoms and signs that will help you realize when you are procrastinating:

- You usually fill your day with low priority tasks.
- Reading e-mails over and over again without even knowing how to start working on them or what you should be doing with them.
- Skipping an item on your to-do list for a long period of time, although you know that it is important.
- Sitting down before your computer or your desk to start doing a high priority task and you almost instantly goes off to make a cup of tea or take your phone out.
- Regularly accepting unimportant tasks that others would like you to do, and you spend your time on these instead of working on with the important ones that are already on your list.
- Usually waiting for the right time or the right mood to do the essential task at hand.

B.   ESTABLISH WHY YOU PROCRASTINATE

Understanding the "why" behind your procrastination moves you closer to overcoming it. Let's say you are putting off cleaning your house. Maybe it's because you've allowed it to get so out of hand that it's become overwhelming to you and you just wish it would go away. Usually, procrastination takes place whenever a task that needs to be done is not pleasurable. Most humans have no problem with getting things done that's pleasurable to them. It's human nature. We are designed to move away from pain and draw close to pleasure.

- An unpleasant or boring job could sometimes be the reason for your procrastination because you try to avoid it. To resolve this, finish them quickly so that you can proceed and focus on the more pleasurable aspects of the task. Break this large tasks down into smaller tasks you can do back to back.
- Another reason could be because you are not organized. The best way to deal with this is to make and prioritize your own to-do lists and schedules.
- Perfectionists are usually procrastinators for they tend to think they do not have enough skills or resources to do the task perfectly, so they end up to not doing it at all.

4 EASY STEPS TO COUNTER PROCRASTINATION

1. Mind shifting: since we recognize that humans are wired to move away from painful things, try associating procrastination with the consequences of not getting important things done. Create a mental picture of the negative results that can occur if you don't get things done. This mental shift can give you the motivation to take action in order to avoid the pain of the consequences.

2. Prioritize: Sometimes you may procrastinate because it seems like there's so much to do yet so little time to get things done. A way to overcome this type of procrastination is through prioritizing. Write down a "to-do" list and then look it over to see what tasks are most important and what tasks are least important. Then prioritize those tasks according to their importance level (1 being the most important while 10 being the least important, or vice-versa) .

3. Accountability Partner: Appointing someone to hold you accountable is another great way to combat procrastination. We usually attempt to do what we say when we know that someone else is watching us and will hold us accountable.

4. Plan ahead: This step can tie into step 2. Establish your priority "to do" list the night before. Accomplishing your list ahead of time can, first of all,

give you a boost of confidence since you've gotten something done. You may also find yourself sleeping better at night looking forward to the next day. Since we cannot predict with certainty the events of tomorrow, be prepared to change some things around on your list if need be.

Procrastination is a habit that is hard to kill. Here are helpful motivating factors for you to get moving forward:

- You need to make up your own rewards, like promising yourself some dessert if you have finished a certain task. Make sure you become aware of how good it feels to complete things.
- Peer pressure does really work. You may ask a friend or a co-worker to check up on you. This is said to be the principle behind self-help groups, and this is generally renowned as a highly effective approach.
- You should spot the consequences of not doing the chore.

CHAPTER TWO

WHY DO WE PROCRASTINATE?

How many times have you avoided cleaning your closet reasoning with yourself about other important tasks that you may have to do or convincing yourself how cleaning is not 'significant' enough to be completed at this point in time? Congratulations, for you, are procrastinating the task. And hey, welcome to the club. It must be good to hear that you are not the only one. Well, here's some more good news. There are millions of procrastinators all around the world. Scratch that – more like billions. Now it's time for the bad part. If not acted upon, then procrastination can very well affect your productivity, your efficiency and even your ability to function normally in your day to day life if it isn't already.

THE COMMON SYMPTOMS

A procrastinator often spends up more energy in putting off a task than what he or she would have spent in completing it. The mind gives constant reminders about the task and a person will try his or her best to put the thoughts away, often eating up one's own positive energy resource. Such thoughts can not only be an energy drainer but can also weigh down heavily on the confidence of a person. In simple terms, procrastination is nothing but self-sabotage.

TYPES OF PROCRASTINATORS

Here's some more juicy insight, such as the different types of procrastinators. The first category is relaxed procrastinators and the second is tense-afraid procrastinators. I think the names are pretty self-explanatory, but here's a detailed description.

- A tense-afraid procrastinator will usually avoid a task because he/she is too tense to handle the stress that the task may bring about. At times, he or she is confused about the importance of the task and is unable to prioritize these tasks in life. In most cases, this leads to further procrastination. For example, studying for an examination. He or she will be too worried about not being able to complete the studies and will, in turn, make frequent trips to the washroom, drink coffee, scroll through social media and end up delaying the actual task further.
- The relaxed procrastinator, on the other hand, avoids a task only because he or she doesn't care. They focus their energy on other more enjoyable tasks. A prime example in teens is when they procrastinate their studies but do not do the same with their social lives. It's just a matter of diverting the energy within the

body to something more enjoyable, such as playing video games.

Procrastination is a problem that many of us face. Almost everyone has their particular issues that cause people to delay. Unfortunately, 20% of the population identifies themselves as chronic procrastinators. These are only the individuals that identify themselves as this as well. Remember, the first part of controlling procrastination is realizing that there is a problem in the first place. Many of these individuals don't ever get to the realization part, because no one is there to tell them or they just don't see a need to change. There are so many great goals that people have, and procrastination keeps them from achieving those goals.

WHY DO PEOPLE PROCRASTINATE?

Procrastinators can be broken down into different types and different combinations of these types. People even go through stages with different forms of procrastination depending on what is happening. Their actions follow particular plans and for most procrastinators there is something they need.

HOW DO PEOPLE PROCRASTINATE?

The chronic delay is not typically a problem of time management or planning. The problem is finding distractions that can delay work but do not require a lot of commitment. Examples would be checking email or organizing things that are not important. The problem is actually chronic avoidance. You are avoiding taking productive action.

WHAT ARE THE CONSEQUENCES?

The obvious is that things that need to get completed either do not get done or they are done in a hurry. Sometimes when things are done at the last minute, you do not take the time to make your best effort, which is reflected in your work. This can, in the end, cost you jobs, grades, relationships and more.

CAN FRIENDS HELP ME STOP PROCRASTINATING?

Often times procrastination includes creating plenty of excuses that friends and family may allow which continues the cycle. You can ask those you care about to be firm when you break your schedules and mini goals. This would help you, but even then they may be soft when you do not complete what you need.

WHAT CAN I DO TO STOP PROCRASTINATING?

The easiest way to not procrastinate is to learn about your procrastination style and what it is you need. The second is to put your darn phone down. Lock it in another room and forget about it. Also, you can sit alone, in a quiet space and ask yourself why you procrastinate. Then listen for an answer. Ask yourself what is the advantage, and again wait and listen for an answer. Ask what you need to do to stop procrastinating and listen. Your body knows the answers and those answers may surprise you. Once you know the problems it will be easier to stop your procrastination and start doing.

Do you procrastinate because of...?

1. Fear of failure or success
2. Fear of rejection
3. Lack of knowledge on how to proceed
4. You don't like the task
5. Lack of time

Once you understand why you are procrastinating you can design a plan of action. If you are afraid of failure or rejection, just grab the bull by the horns and complete the task to the best of your ability. Design a step-by-step system on how to complete the task. If you do not have the required knowledge, seek out the guidance of a friend or a coach. Together you can work on completing the task. If you do not like to perform the task or do not have the time to complete it, consider hiring someone or asking for help to complete the task. If you REALLY don't have the time, then consider whether or not your other tasks are just as, if not more important.

Once the task is completed or delegated, you will feel a sense of accomplishment. You will be growing personally and a professional. So, stop procrastinating. Stop talking and start doing. Take Action.

WHY DO PEOPLE CHOOSE TO PROCRASTINATE?

Now, we all procrastinate from time to time. It's only when procrastination stops or hinders us from leading a full and vibrant life that it becomes a problem.

Some of us procrastinate at work with admin tasks, while some of us at home with household chores. Did you know that a form of procrastination is not paying your bills on time? (Assuming you have the means to do so). People may miss job or promotion opportunities; they may not appeal against parking fines on time or they may leave their Christmas or birthday gift shopping until the last minute. These are all real forms of procrastination and the consequences are always worse.

Procrastinators may tell themselves "I'll do this tomorrow" or "I work best under pressure." But the truth is procrastinators may put off doing things indefinitely - how many times have you heard someone say "I'll go on a diet tomorrow."? There are many ways to disrupt our lives but one of the worst ways, in my opinion, is procrastination. After all, who wants a life full of regrets through not taking action on time?

It is generally thought that we learn to procrastinate rather than we are born with it. Procrastination can be learned from one's parents, siblings or other figures of authority as we are growing up.

It is sometimes a response to an authoritarian parenting style. Having controlling parents may keep children from developing the ability to take immediate action without seeking some extra guidance from an authority figure in their lives. As we then become adults we may still be seeking that extra guidance before we act, but at this point, the authority figures may not be present, which in turn leads us to put off or defer taking action.

In some cases, procrastination may be a form of rebellion or even a way of simply being noticed. Procrastinators may turn to friends rather than family for support, but unfortunately, our friends may actually justify the problem by accepting our excuses.

There are several effects of procrastination: Health for instance.. Studies have shown that procrastination may lead to a compromised immune system with more colds and flu, as well as more gastrointestinal problems and insomnia.

Procrastination may also shift the burden of responsibility away from us and onto others, and in doing so leads to resentfulness and may destroy teamwork and our relationships.

THERE ARE A NUMBER OF DIFFERENT TYPES OF PROCRASTINATORS:

1. Those seeking a high – these individuals leave things to the last minute and get a buzz from frantic last minute activities - especially when they have no options
2. Those with a fear of failure - The may even fear success, but either way this fear holds them back from the action. They may also be self-conscious and worry about what others may think of them.
3. Those who simply want to avoid making decisions. In this way, they take no responsibility for the outcome.

Now, if you're like me, and want to get rid of procrastination from your life completely, there are a number of techniques available, which we will cover later.

With concentrated effort, it is possible for procrastinators to beat their procrastination on their own. It will take a lot of mental energy and can be very draining. However, just because it's difficult, doesn't mean it's not worth it.

Don't procrastinate on getting rid of your procrastination habits!

CHAPTER THREE

WAYS TO STOP PROCRASTINATING NOW

1. Procrastination emancipation: Once you've fully understood that one of the biggest reasons you have been procrastinating is that you're focusing only on finishing (and that's too daunting) you'll begin to instead concentrate on starting, which is a much more approachable and manageable way to get the thing done. All you need to do is keep starting, and finishing will take care of itself.
2. Procrastination transformation: Nothing helps you achieve more easily than knowing all the steps you need to take, having a plan to take them, scheduling that plan into your calendar, creating incentives to make following through more attractive (and consequences to make it less attractive!), and putting some accountability supports into place. This, combined with a simple procrastination meditation, will get you back on track quickly and easily.
3. Procrastination consultation: Talk with friends about how they overcame procrastination. Buddy up with them on their own projects, holding each other accountable to get things done. Hire a procrastination

coach, someone who has worked with hundreds of people and not only knows about procrastination generation but has helped many veteran procrastinators with procrastination renunciation.

4. Procrastination exploration: What is your procrastination costing you? Do you have a procrastination reputation? Do you continually have to make procrastination explanations or reparations to others? Are you in procrastination isolation so nobody will know what you're not doing? Is your credit history in procrastination degradation because of paying bills late? Are you in procrastination desperation because you might lose your job or significant relationships? Sometimes understanding how badly you're paying and in exactly what ways can provoke you to seek assistance.

5. Procrastination perspiration: You may think that the only way to stop procrastinating is to use willpower and discipline. While that certainly can work, it can cost you a lot of energy and struggle.

6. By allowing yourself to begin recognizing what is specifically in the way of following through and creating simple new patterns, progress can be pretty painless and immediate.

7. Procrastination inclination: At the moment you are about to procrastinate, stop for just a moment to acknowledge the pattern, even if you continue on to

put off whatever you were going to do. Awareness and acceptance that these are your current patterns is a necessary step in procrastination extermination.

8. Procrastination alienation: Recognize that you're not alone, and are, in fact, in excellent company. Most people procrastinate about something, sometimes about many things. In a recent survey on procrastination, almost 1/3 of respondents who identified themselves as procrastinators had a post-graduation or higher education.

9. Procrastination temptation: If you hang out with people who coax you to procrastinate, it's time to start surrounding yourself with better examples. If you know that certain situations are too enticing and will lure you from following through, create a workaround plan that will help you prevent yourself from "taking the bait".

10. Procrastination exaggeration: Are you really procrastinating, or are you simply focusing on other priorities? It's possible that those things you're not doing shouldn't get done until sometime later, perhaps not at all. Focus on only the most significant areas first, and the rest will come.

11. Procrastination condemnation: Lose the labels! All those things you call yourself, such as lazy, scattered, disorganized, not good enough, incompetent, or stupid, for example, aren't helping you get things

done, are they? You've learned to believe them, and you think they've become something of a self-fulfilling prophecy. If you look around yourself, though, you'll see evidence that you can accomplish quite a number of things without delay.

HOW TO BEAT PROCRASTINATION USING THIS 3-STEP PROCESS

You can literally say, "Goodbye Procrastination". Now, that might sound too simple, but it really is that simple; simple but very effective! What I'm suggesting is that you learn to "Externalize It!"

TRY THIS 3-STEP PROCESS TO EXTERNALIZE, ELIMINATE, & DETERMINE

1. EXTERNALIZE PROCRASTINATION

Externalizing, in the therapeutic sense, means to make a mental projection, in image form, outside of oneself, and it is a method for counseling that is used in Narrative Therapy. It is a very useful therapeutic 'tool' for reducing self-blame and allows clients to create space for re-framing and restructuring self-identity. Therapists and counselors alike may tailor their use of externalization for a much broader spectrum.

We don't often call it by name directly, more often we indirectly speak of or think about it (i.e., "I should do this, but..." or "I can't seem to get to that project, maybe later...") only to wonder "why" we can't follow through and accomplish our goals. We know we "hate it" and "want it gone," but it seems that we surely haven't become great experts when it comes to saying goodbye to it for good.

So, if you view Procrastination as an entity outside yourself...someone else or something else...it can greatly help you to get past the feelings of "I am a 'bad' procrastinator" or something of the like. When you externalize, you essentially relieve yourself of the burden because the "Procrastinator" or "Procrastination" is outside yourself...It is NOT YOU! So, that means that the next time you find yourself struggling with your time management and feel procrastination is directing your actions, you can stop blaming yourself and sabotaging your belief in yourself to change your behaviors. You are not "The Procrastinator" and "The Procrastinator" is not your identity! Period.

Perhaps look at it like this: "I am learning now that procrastination can no longer be in my life and my choices will not be made to benefit procrastination anymore!

I am me and it has to leave now!" Make a mental picture of procrastination (create a specific vision in your mind) and watch procrastination literally walk through a doorway and out of your life."

Externalizing "Procrastination" allows you to release it and the inner grip that it once had on you. Procrastination does not have to be your resident arch nemesis any longer. If you try viewing it as separate from yourself, can begin to have the upper hand, free of the frustration it brought with it. However, the work doesn't stop here...

2.   ELIMINATE RESISTANCE

Once you decide to release it, you need to begin to eliminate its companion, which is resistance. Much of your procrastinating behavior is grounded in 'mental resistance,' so it makes sense to find a way to create space for a new mindset. You can even repeat Step 1 now and externalize "Resistance" ("It" now has a name, too). Let it go out the same doorway as procrastination!

The bottom line is: You've been battling two fierce opponents and it seems that the more any of us 'resist' the more we procrastinate, and the stronger "Resistance and Procrastination" become, taking over our very existence. So, how do you fight off resistance?

Start using affirmations to help you eliminate resistance. Use your words and create an action to accomplish this. For instance, you could say, "I am no longer allowing resistance and procrastination to rent space in my head and use up my mental energy," or, "I am watching resistance and procrastination leave me now". Or, you might take a slightly different approach and say, "I am free to choose procrastination and resistance as friends (or perhaps teachers) so that I can learn more about why they held me back and why I fought with them and myself to get things done!"

Also, to eliminate resistance, you need to become aware of its presence. It's sneaky if you're not paying attention. Resistance will make your body feel terrible. Any response you have to a negative feeling is your body's attempt to send you the "red flag" that it is in motion. What you may or may not realize is that you get to control your "resistance gauge" and if you don't want it, you can let your thoughts overcome it.

Again, use your words and say, "I am feeling anxious right now, and that tells me that resistance is trying to come back into my life. There isn't room for you, Resistance. I am at peace here without you." The more you say it, and believe it, and feel it, the more you can lower that heartbeat and your anxiety will start to dissipate.

Taken a step further, resistance is a by-product of fear. Fear is not as easy to externalize, so we need to expand the search for answers by looking at the underlying fear that initiated your resistance that resulted in allowing procrastination and resistance to rent space in your mind.

3.   DETERMINE YOUR FEAR

Begin to ask yourself what you felt the last time resistance led to procrastinating behavior. Did you feel anxious, afraid, confused, frustrated, or angry? Maybe all of the above? Think about this and really try to dig deep into the process of your procrastinating behavior. Step three is an important piece of this puzzle, so start by considering these three questions:

1. Am I fearful of rejection by others if I follow through with this goal or task?
2. Am I fearful of not knowing all the answers going in, so it's better to lack the initiative than it is to attempt and fail?
3. Am I fearful of letting go of Procrastination because it has protected me and if I freely give up something that has become valuable to me, won't I feel lost without it?

This should jump-start personal self reflection if you really want to look to the source of your fear. Remember: "Your fear is what led to your resistance that enabled procrastination." It's never an easy process to look inside and become acutely aware of negative emotions and behaviors. But, if you start this process by letting go of your identity as "The Procrastinator" or "A Procrastinator," you've made the first giant step in learning to "Externalize, Eliminate and Determine" your way to success.

CHAPTER FOUR

IS IT LAZINESS?

I for one am guilty of procrastination and used to think of myself as lazy. However, one evening as I lay on the sofa and I recounted my very busy day in my head - I needed that justification for having not started my very important writing assignment. I realized that in essence, I was not lazy at all.

In my search for answers, the one thing that I did discover is that I am not alone. I have been closely observing my friends an family and discovered that most people procrastinate to some degree or other. The degree at which people procrastinate varies from the most chronic procrastinator who never seems to achieve anything - for a variety of 'good' reasons real or unreal, to the mild procrastinator who can at least admit and notice when procrastination is taking place and do something about it.

WHY DO WE PUT OFF IMPORTANT TASKS THROUGH PROCRASTINATION?

I found this to be most perplexing. My task was important to me, I was eager and keen - yet I found I was never in the right mood; the place was too messy, or I had things to do. The phone is ringing and I had better answer it or... or what? Why was I making everything else so much more important than that what I wanted to do?

The dictionary definition of procrastination is the act of postponing, delaying or putting off, especially out of habitual carelessness or laziness.

So, basically procrastination refers to the act of replacing high-priority actions with tasks of low-priority, and so putting off important tasks to a later time. This is exactly what I was doing; I wasn't being lazy after all! Or was I?

A procrastinator needs to address 'why the task is being put off'. The identifying reason alone will be the motivating force to take action and complete the task at hand. In essence, procrastination is a thief of time.

Time management experts may say write a 'to do list' and tick them off as you go. However, if you are like me, I can tick off things and still avoid the one thing that was really important to do because obviously, it can go on tomorrow's list. Yet when tomorrow comes another day dawns, and other things still always seem to take priority.

Procrastinators are not born this way. They are made over the course of time. The procrastination habit can be learned within the family and in the school of life. But I believe not directly, it is a learned action more by submitting to a pressure or a fear of failure.

Learned behaviors can be unlearned, so procrastinators can change - one small step at a time.

Why do we attach 'no importance' to very important tasks?

Believe it or not, procrastinators actually tell lies to themselves. They do not see themselves in their true light; they say things like "I'll feel more like doing this tomorrow." Or "I'll work best after a good night's sleep." But in reality, they do not get the urge the next day or work best after rest. Plus, they justify themselves by saying "this isn't really that important". Procrastinators can actually squander their resources. When you put something off once, it makes it that much easier to do it again.

There are many ways to self-sabotage your success in life and procrastination is one choice of the path that people take without even realizing they are doing it. Procrastinating behavior can be actions taken to avoid the fear of failure or even fear of success. Some procrastinators are very concerned with what others think of them; they would rather have others think they lack effort, rather than ability. By not making decisions, procrastinators absolve themselves of the responsibility for the outcome of events. This was exactly what my personal problem was, and it wasn't easy to overcome.

There can be big costs to procrastination. Health is one, as well as a productive life. Procrastination can lead to guilt, stress, and insomnia, which can, in turn, lead to severe loss of personal productivity as well strain in personal relationships. It has a tendency to shift the burden of responsibilities onto others, who may then become resentful. Therefore, it is very important to try to modify or reduce this behavior as much as possible and as soon as possible.

You can change this prevailing and self-sabotaging behavior with a few simple steps.

Traditionally, procrastination has been associated with the following tendencies:

- Perfectionism, which is a tendency to negatively evaluate outcomes and one's own performance.
- An intense fear and avoidance of evaluation of one's abilities by others.
- Heightened social self-consciousness and anxiety,
- Recurrent low mood.

Exploring why you procrastinate is the first step towards a transformation. There can be many reasons for example; fear, dislike, pressure, boredom, and avoidance of responsibility. This habit has been developed over a long period of time, so the change will take time too. You can change your behavior; just don't expect to change it overnight.

You can experiment with different strategies as the same strategy does not work for everyone.

Try some of these useful tips:

- Break down large tasks or projects into smaller chunks.
- Reward yourself for small successes - you deserve it
- Do not punish yourself when you do procrastinate. You will eventually develop new habits with new feelings of self-confidence and achievement. Instead, ask yourself if the consequence of procrastinating was really worth it.
- If you are finding this to be difficult, then you know it's worth doing. Enlist the help of an 'Anti-Procrastinator Coach' who is typically a close good friend you have confided in who will alert you when they find you procrastinating.

- Start on your important task of the day FIRST and follow on later with all those other less important tasks of the day.

In brief, most procrastinators are not lazy but have the ability to do all sorts of other tasks in order to put off the most 'important task' of the day. This is accomplished for a variety of reasons, most of which are not reasons but excuses. Being a self-confessed procrastinator myself, I know it is not always intentional, and in some cases subconscious, but once it is recognized you now have the ability to stop in your tracks and set it straight.

In my opinion, the way to 'solve' the problem of procrastination is to enjoy the pull of achievement by not putting off the 'important task' but by putting off the 'less important tasks' that can be left undone. These feelings of achievement are the feelings that will help you drive the changes to your behavior.

So, stop procrastinating and take action and start doing. As Alexander Graham Bell once said, "The only difference between success and failure is the ability to take action."

CHAPTER FIVE

HOW TO END PROCRASTINATION

1.   TIME MANAGEMENT

If you're struggling with procrastination, you know that you want to end the struggle and overcome it. I know you think you're not good at time management. Procrastination is wrecking your life, whether you know it or not. If not wrecking, then hindering your ability to be the best and most efficient version of yourself.

These strategies, followed in order and really put to use, will help you overcome your procrastination.

What you'll learn is that it's not really all about time management. Procrastination is a mental block, a paralysis that takes hold of us and makes us think we're lazy and worthless when in reality we're none of those things.

That's what makes these strategies so powerful. They get to the root of the procrastination and eliminates it so you can go forward as a person with a purpose.

1. Identify what's going on: It may be procrastination. You may be putting things off without a good reason. On the other hand, you may have very good reasons

for changing the time and order when you do things. You may be ill, or you may be changing priorities. You may be waiting on someone else. Or, you may have just decided something doesn't need doing. None of that is procrastination. But if you are procrastinating, you can do something about it.

2. Relax: Although what you're experiencing is stressful, it is important that you find a way to relax and stop letting the stress build up. Stress only leads to more procrastination. Take some time to just not think about time management, procrastination or any of the difficulties you're facing because of this burden.

3. Do triage: Be very honest with yourself about what you have outstanding, what you can complete and what you can't complete. This will not be easy but it is very, very necessary. If you're like me and 99% of the people I work with, there are things you can't complete on your current list. Being honest about this is the most important step in time management procrastination elimination. Wow, say that five times fast..

4. Release: Let go of the projects you cannot complete. This may be unpleasant, but the hard part won't take long and you'll be free to go on to the next step, which is much more pleasant and much easier.

5. Reaffirm: Now you need to recommit to the projects and tasks you can and will complete. At this point,

you're just making a commitment, but soon you'll figure out how to get all of it done.

6. Strategize: Create a time management procrastination avoidance plan that will help you get everything done without procrastinating.

7. Implement: Now put your plan into action and go forward as a person who does not procrastinate.

These strategies will help you become a person who avoids procrastination before it even begins.

2.   HYPNOSIS

Another way to treat and end procrastination once and for all is to train your mind to work with the subconscious where permanent changes are activated and self-sabotaging thoughts and behaviors are eliminated for good. Procrastination Hypnosis is a unique, yet innovative approach to ending procrastination that does just that.

How can Procrastination Hypnosis solve your procrastination problem? To fully appreciate this, indulge in some positive procrastination to understand why you procrastinate and are so jolly lazy, lying around doing diddly squat, wasting time and ignoring the chores. This is okay for a bit, but the real danger is when it becomes a way of life.

Has it got to stage with you yet? Are you chronically lazy, putting things off, don't pay the bills on time or even worse, stay in a job you HATE? Procrastinators waste time doing nothing even though they are well aware that things need doing. But for some reason, they just don't do it. Then the snowballing effect wacks you in the back of your head and tiny tasks become massive. What a travesty this an become if you don't make the effort to get over yourself and end procrastination. You can miss out on so much of life. Is that what you want?

Ave you ever been told you're lazy, a waste of space, ineffective or unreliable? Hmm, perhaps not to your face? Failure to deal with procrastination stands between you and a productive, fuller life and only launches you further along the downward, spiraling slide to an empty, unfulfilling life where frustration and powerlessness is your constant companion.

HOW TO PROCRASTINATION HYPNOSIS CAN END PROCRASTINATION

This is an effective way is to make your mind aware of and deal with it on a subconscious level by reprogramming your thought patterns and eliminating sabotaging behaviors. It's a proven treatment for procrastination that eliminates it for good.

The reason this works so effectively is that chronic procrastination or laziness is a psychological issue that is often deeply ingrained over many years. Procrastination Hypnosis makes changes at the subconscious level, eliminates deeply ingrained patterns and ends procrastination for good. Additionally, it's surprisingly simple.

This change at the subconscious level is the solution to reprogramming your mind and setting it back on course. As Neil Armstrong's small step on the moon was a huge step for mankind, this small step could be a huge leap for your new improved life from here on out.

THE EFFECTS OF HYPNOSIS

There is truly no need to continue on the procrastination cycle of a wait, wait, wait, stress out, and wait some more. You can overcome procrastination. How? Through the power of hypnosis.

Hypnosis is not some hocus pocus form of psychotherapy - it is simply a naturally occurring state of mind that bypasses the conscious part of the mind. When the conscious is bypassed, we don't pass judgment on what is being suggested.

Believe it or not, we are in a hypnotic state quite often. For instance, here are some times when you have "turned off" the judgment portion of your mind:

When you see a commercial on TV that influences you to buy a product.

When an expert tells you something and you don't question the validity of that statement.

Children do it when they are pretending.

By going around the judgment portion of the mind, suggestions can be put into your subconscious and lead you towards a particular goal - just the way advertisers propel you towards their product.

Hypnosis can help you overcome procrastination forever. How? By detouring around your conscious mind!

Procrastination is nothing more than a bad habit. Your conscious mind doesn't like change and will "talk" you right out of changing. However, if you can get those suggestions into your subconscious mind without the judgmental filter, you can change from being a procrastinator to being an achiever.

Hypnosis and meditation is stronger than willpower because it puts the suggestions straight into your subconscious, the way advertisers do. By the time the suggestions reach your conscious mind, they will have already been accepted by your subconscious - so no more defeating self-talk to contend with!

Best of all, your changed status from procrastinator to achiever means that you will achieve your goals and still have time left over. Instead of using up all your spare time with worry, guilt, and frustration, you can use your spare time for enjoyment and relaxation!

THE WAY I SEE IT, YOU'VE GOT TWO OPTIONS;

a. Let life control you by doing nothing. Continue along the path to an empty, unfulfilled life full of frustration and feelings of powerlessness because you won't make the decision to take the necessary action to end your procrastination problem.
b. Take control of your life. Get a grip on yourself, beat procrastination and create a life you actually want instead of allowing life to control you by default.

Procrastination is a killer - a killer of dreams, ambitions, and achievement.

My question to you, is what are you going to do now?

CHAPTER SIX

FIVE EMPOWERING PROCRASTINATION TIPS

One of the most destructive effects of procrastination is the fact that it makes you feel out of control. Procrastination is like an invisible force that keeps you from doing the very things you know you must do. With the increasing demands on our time and attention, there seems to be an increase in procrastination as a chronic problem, especially amongst those people that want to succeed the most. Procrastination usually sets in when you feel overwhelmed by all the 'have to's' in life, and instead of making steady progress you take on too much without ever getting any of it done.

Feeling out of control takes away all your power to shape and direct your own life. It's true that there are many things over which you have no control, but you always have full control over what you ultimately become - and what really happens to you is a mental process independent of the circumstances and events of the outside world. Being empowered means that you realize that you already have the power and this realization also gives you the ability to take action. Here are five empowering procrastination tips that can help you to reach this realization and become empowered to effectively deal with procrastination and inaction.

1.   IT'S ALL INTERNAL

Procrastination is an internal process and although it might feel like it's happening to you, you are in fact responsible for it. This procrastination tip can help to put you back in control almost immediately. Procrastination is not an external force, but an internal response and evaluation. The simple realization that it's 'you' that's doing it to 'you', gives you the power to do something about it.

2.   IT'S ALL YOU

When procrastination drags you down, it's all too easy to think that 'it just is what it is' and that you can't do anything about it. Although it feels like you have no control, you actually do. In fact, this is why you feel out of control - because you believe that you can't do anything about it. There are two very important beliefs you need to develop to help you break free from procrastination.

The first is that you CAN overcome procrastination and the second is that YOU can overcome procrastination. No one else can do it for you and because you created it; you can un-create it.

3.   IT'S ALL IN YOUR HEAD

The reason why most people remain stuck in patterns of procrastination is that of fear. At the most fundamental level, all forms of procrastination come down to fear, and the anxiety that stems from that fear. What you don't face ultimately controls you. To overcome the fear and the procrastination that comes with it, you need to confront and do the very things you don't want to do. The instant you do, you take charge and it no longer has any control over you. The ironic thing is that fear only exists in your imagination - it's always something that hasn't happened yet. Procrastination is not real - it's only the way you evaluate fear in your mind.

4.   IT'S ALL ABOUT CONDITIONING

Success at anything in life relies on consistency. The best of the best at anything are those who can repeat their greatness consistently. The way you become consistent is through conditioning. Your nervous system operates through conditioning. When you do something over and over again it becomes 'normal' and when it's normal you don't have to think about it - it becomes automatic. The challenge is that this principle works both ways. Whether your conditioned responses support you or whether it pulls you down, your nervous system does not make that distinction. If procrastination is your conditioned response you will always feel out of control, simply because that's what you've 'learned' to do automatically. You simply need to 'recondition' yourself to a new response; to teach yourself to respond in a different way...

5.   IT'S ALL ABOUT AWARENESS

Procrastination does serve a purpose - and a very important one at that, but only if you are aware of the benefits. We only procrastinate about those things that have value to us. At some level, either directly or indirectly, you believe that taking action will benefit you. If it didn't it wouldn't bother you, right? Be grateful for procrastination and use it as a guide to 'know' what you need to act upon.

Being aware of this fact, and developing awareness of what you do and fail to do can empower you to be in charge of yourself on a much higher level.

When you are empowered you are in charge, and even if things seem to go wrong on the surface, underneath you know that you have the power to deal with it effectively on your on terms. Procrastination is disempowering and it takes away your ability to take immediate action and deal with any situation. Always remember that you are ultimately in charge of you. Tomorrow will be today, tomorrow. Don't delay. Act!

CHAPTER SEVEN

MANY NEGATIVE EFFECTS OF PROCRASTINATION

The Negative Effects of Procrastination take place in all of your major life areas:

Relationships with Your Spouse or Significant Other

Relationships with Your Children

Work or Business

Health

Finances

How are each of these areas affected by your lack of action?

Let's take a look at 5 areas of your life and how procrastinating affects it.

A.   ADVERSE EFFECTS OF RELATIONSHIPS WITH YOUR SPOUSE OR SIGNIFICANT OTHER

You love your partner. You truly do, but do they know it?

Do you keep thinking that you should send them flowers, take them to dinner or do something nice just because?

Do you promise that you will do stuff together and you just never get around to it?

Do you promise that you will complete your house to-do list but you keep putting it off?

If you answered yes to any of these questions, I want you to think. What are you doing to your relationship with your significant other?

Maybe they are irritated with you. Then, you become irritated with them.

What could be the big negative effect of procrastination? You break up. Now, if you're not married, you might think that's no big deal. There are other fish in the sea and so on and so forth. Really?

What happens when you do the same thing to your next partner? Now, if you are married, think about the expense and stress of an escalated event.

B. NEGATIVE SIDE EFFECTS OF PROCRASTINATION IN RELATIONSHIPS WITH YOUR CHILDREN

If you don't have kids, skip this one and go to the next section. If you do have kids, what kind of example are you setting for them? They see you putting stuff off so why wouldn't they put their chores and school work off?

Now, what happens if you have procrastinated in setting up your will and you pass away?

If you have loads of debt because you put off getting your finances in order, what kind of legacy are you leaving them behind? People don't think about these things because they are unpleasant. However, it's beneficial to do so.

C. DEBILITATING EFFECTS OF YOUR BUSINESS

You know there are a few things you must do in your business in order for it to grow or even get started.

For me, they are meeting people, putting out content, and communicating with my list. There are other things too, but nothing will happen if I don't do those three basic things.

Now, imagine you decided you'll just do that basic task tomorrow. When you finally do get around to it, how many days did you waste? Is it a month later?

How the heck are you going to build a business if you can't even hold yourself to do the bare minimum?

Don't let this be you.

D. HOW DOES PROCRASTINATION AFFECT YOUR HEALTH?

What if you have skipped having your regular checkups? Then, one day, God forbid, you find something. The doctor tells you that either it's too late or that you need to schedule something quickly.

Don't continue to put off eating healthy or exercising until tomorrow. What if tomorrow doesn't come? It's hard to think about but these are real scenarios. No one ever thinks it will happen to them until it does.

E. NEGATIVE EFFECTS OF PROCRASTINATION ON YOUR FINANCES

Imagine you keep saying that you will pay your bills tomorrow. Now, mind you, you do have the money, but you just keep procrastinating on paying them.

Some of those late payment fees can be upwards of 35 bucks! How much a month are you paying because of your procrastination?

So what do you do now?

I suggest you write down five things that you have been procrastinating on in each area of your life.

Then, set some time aside and do them.

Make a game out of it. How?

Put on a song and see how far or how much you can do in one of your areas affected by procrastinating.

Get a buddy. Tell someone what you are going to do and have them hold you accountable.

Those are just a few suggestions of how to get rid of the negative effects of procrastination. Brainstorm and find some more. Procrastination can really destroy your life if you let it.

STOP PROCRASTINATION AND SUCCEED

No matter who you are, it happens to the best of us. We can all make excuses for not doing what we know we should do or want to do. Procrastination can affect us all. New Year's resolutions are all well and good if you achieve them. Many people find that they are no further ahead this year with their aims and ambitions than they were last year.

If you have felt that nagging sense that things are the same and the positive changes you crave don't happen, you may be suffering from the habit of procrastination.

A.   PROCRASTINATION IN YOUR OCCUPATION

Are you someone who is always late to work or appointments because your motivation is missing. Do you lose hours at work doing non-essential jobs and avoid getting going with the tasks you know you should be doing? A vicious cycle can start for you. The more you delay starting that new project or priority task, the more pressure you will feel and the more likely you are to avoid it and procrastinate. Some people even change employers and jobs to avoid having to start or complete a project that they have prevaricated over.

You may be bored in your current job but the security of it keeps you from leaving and you feel trapped. The fear of what a new job might involve may stop you from applying for new jobs and getting a role that could re-motivate you. All the time you delay, your self-confidence is being eroded and your ability to procrastinate grows.

B. PERSONAL LIFE PROCRASTINATION

Have you stayed in your relationship because it provides familiarity and a sense of safety? Has your relationship lost its spark and you and your partner have settled into a safe and yet boring rut? This can happen in any relationship and it doesn't mean that you have to end it. The best relationship for you may be the one that you are currently in. Unless you are present in the relationship and appreciate it, you may feel unhappy, lost or just trapped. Procrastination can become of feature of personal relationships too.

C.   DOMESTIC PROCRASTINATION

Are the numbers of domestic jobs at home building up? Does your home need some repair or maintenance such as a cupboard that needs fixing or a leaky pipe that needs to be repaired? Sometimes even calling in a contractor to fix a domestic problem can lead to procrastination. Instead of it being a simple job, not fixing it in time makes for a more expensive repair in the future. You may have outstanding bills that you have not settled or other legal or challenging matters that need your attention but you have yet to tackle them.

Your home should be a place where you can unwind and relax, yet you may find that your home is no longer that safe and secure haven. The unstated or unfinished jobs around your home just add to a sense of drift as the years go by and nothing changes.

Procrastination can have a negative affect on many areas of our lives. Yet, you don't have to keep putting up with a life of malaise. If you envy others' success, it means you recognize things can be different and you can change too. Yet, procrastination is often just a state of mind that anyone can fall victim to and recover from.

Maybe you have tried and (apparently) failed to change before. Maybe you have convinced yourself that whatever you do, nothing will improve for you. There is a common negative saying that you may be familiar with: "I should accept my lot". If you have used it yourself then stop it now. It doesn't serve you in any way other than to keep you trapped as you are. Don't use it as a justification for misfortunes.

STOP YOUR PROCRASTINATION

Understanding procrastination can also provide the clues to escaping from it too. Initially, take things one step at a time. Don't put pressure on yourself by aiming for too many goals. This approach can overwhelm you. Keep it simple to start with and aim for tasks, goals, and achievements that are easy for you. Small and easy goals are more likely to be achieved. In reaching your sense of success, no matter how small, you are more likely to then be able to achieve bigger and longer term goals.

Start today by viewing yourself differently and quit using any negative self-labels. If you view yourself succeeding and doing those tasks and jobs, you are much more likely to succeed (research has shown this). If you label yourself with names such as useless, lazy, or other unhelpful adjectives, it will undermine your ability to motivate yourself and make those all important changes.

If you change how you imagine yourself to be, and drop the negative labels, you will find it easier to make progress.

Procrastination is not something you neccesarily inherited, but something that may have been influenced by others. Procrastination is a habit but it doesn't have to be a way of life.

As human beings, we are very adaptable and change habits all the time. Just a little bit of work can support your decision to stop procrastinating. Rather than feeling like a victim of it, take control of your life.

CHAPTER EIGHT

PROCRASTINATION AS A CAREER KILLER

Are you a procrastinator? Do you know a procrastinator? If you're not sure, here are some ways you can tell if you or someone you know is a procrastinator:

There are many reasons that a person may procrastinate, such as:

1. Fear: Anxiety plays a large factor in procrastination. When someone feels anxious about a task it's likely because they think they'll fail, or because they're not quite sure how to approach the task to even begin. The feeling of being overwhelmed comes into play here as well. If the individual feels the task is too large to handle, or they don't have enough time to complete it, they may become overwhelmed with the process, creating a sense of fear.
2. Not knowing where to start: This is quite common among procrastinators. If they don't even know where to start on a project, then they will put the project off as long as possible because they just can't wrap their head around where to begin.

3. Too difficult: The difficulty of the task may vary, but generally the more difficult the task the more likely it'll be put off by a procrastinator. A procrastinator would prefer to complete simpler and more pleasurable activities first to give them the instant satisfaction of a job well done.

So, how can procrastination be a career killer? Here are a few examples:

Consistently completing tasks or projects after the due date can create an impression among supervisors and coworkers that the individual isn't reliable or dependable.

A procrastinator will be overlooked for major projects that could give them an advantage in the workplace because they won't be seen as trustworthy.

Rushing to complete projects at the last minute can cause mistakes, an unfinished or unpolished professional look, and won't be taken lightly by a boss or team member.

Work ethics will be called out if the projects aren't created at a certain level of expectations.

A procrastinator will be viewed as someone who just makes excuses and doesn't create quality work consistently.

Even with just one or two of these examples, a supervisor may choose to use, promote, and applaud others and leave the procrastinator in the dust in regard to increased responsibilities, advancement, raises, and promotions.

HOW DO YOU (OR SOMEONE YOU KNOW) FIX IT?

a. Begin working immediately: create a plan. Figure out the specific steps of what needs to happen to complete the task - and write them down as a plan of action. Creating an action plan will help reduce the fear of tackling the project and will help reduce the procrastination time.

b. Enlist help: Follow-up with a supervisor, team member, or coworker on specific tasks you need help with that they can easily complete. Ask for completion or submission dates for their specific tasks so you know when to expect them. Having assistance will help hold the procrastinator responsible, and will share the weight of the project with others, reducing the anxiety and the fear of failure.

c. Break up the project: don't try tackling the entire project in one shot, especially if it's a large project. Create blocks of tasks that need to be done by a certain date and then list the next steps for the project. This will give the procrastinator a sense of accomplishment as each portion of the project is completed.

d. Be consistent: this is especially true while working with other team members. Show them that you are serious about completing the project on time and with quality. This will help hold everyone accountable, which will produce a much better outcome, and increase the ability to obtain promotions, raises, and recognition.

Procrastination is not something that will be 'cured' overnight. It will take work; it'll be quite frustrating at times, and some things may still slip through the cracks at times. But, as long as you (or the person you know) work at changing the way tasks and projects are handled and are more forward thinking, it'll get easier and easier as you move forward. Just take it one day at a time.

CONCLUSION

Chances are you procrastinate; nearly everyone does, nearly every day (it's one of the few things we don't put off till tomorrow!). Procrastination is a thief, and it's stealing from you on a daily basis. And what it's taking can never, ever be replaced. It steals your time, that most valuable commodity, that thing that's so precious that untold millions couldn't buy you a single minute's worth. Every time you put tasks off until tomorrow, you're letting that time slip away forever. It's time you'll never have again, and it carries opportunities with it, perhaps to never be seen again. Procrastination is the thief of time is an old saying, and a wise one. We would do well to take it to heart.

Many people waste time because they fear failure. For them, to try is to risk failing; therefore, it's easier to never try because then they never fail. You miss 100% of the shots you don't take. In other words, procrastination is saving them from failing. But not really. It's actually causing them to fail because they never try.

Once you figure out the emotional reason behind your procrastination, it's easier to fight. If you know why you waste time, then you either need to overcome that or find another way to satisfy that part of life. For instance, many people procrastinate because they're overworked and need a break. If this is the case, reevaluate your work schedule, you'll get way more done.

The best way to overcome procrastination is to use this emotional reason against yourself. To do this, you need to figure out why you procrastinate and then prove to yourself that procrastinating is causing you more pain or less pleasure depending on how you motivate yourself. While the way you procrastinate will tell you how you're motivated, it's far easier to just ask yourself how you wake up in the morning--are you motivated to get up and enjoy the day or because you really have to pee?

Another major reason for procrastination is a lack of desire. If you don't want to do the task, it's a lot harder to get it done. The real question to ask in that case is why do you put yourself through this? Do you fear the risk of trying something new? Why would you continue doing something you don't like? Because that's key; why do you procrastinate finding other, more enjoyable options for your time? Or, go the other way; work on enjoying what you do.

Procrastination is difficult to manage because we underestimate its accumulative effects and overestimate our ability to handle them. If we cannot eliminate procrastination from our lives entirely, the next best thing is to contain it. This means being aware of our procrastination and taking steps to deal with it. Through constant vigilance, we can manage procrastination effectively and maintain harmony in our lives.

Printed in Great Britain
by Amazon